Communication Guide to Love and Happiness

How to overcome the most common mistakes

I really appreciate you purchasing this book, and I am convinced that you are on the right way. I hope this book will give you helpful tips on how you can create genuine love and intimacy, get trust back into your relationship and become friends again.

Yours, Olivia Lisenchi

We hope you enjoy this book by Olivia Lisenchi. Our goal is to provide high-quality, thought-provoking books and products that connect truth to your real needs and challenges.

The Ocean Publishing

Table of Contents

Introduction

When we first fall in love with someone, it is mostly due to communication. The way we present ourselves to the outside world is a huge part of why we attract the types of partners we end up dating. The way we dress is a form of communication. It speaks to others loudly about us. Whether we want to be seen as sexy, serious, young, sporty, wealthy or part of a gang, our choice of clothing is essential. This also speaks to others about what we value and how we feel about ourselves. Our tone of voice, choice of conversation topics, body language and level of eye contact are all forms of communication. While some of the things we expose are well thought out, we might not even be aware of others.

But besides these tangible aspects, there is also a more subtle, invisible but very strong form of communication. This is unconscious communication. We might be able to tell our friends why we fell for our lover, what we remember about our first date and what we found attractive. But the fact of the matter is that we all have unconscious patterns that we follow. These are intimately linked with our personality, our upbringing, and our psychological development. What this means is that our psyche picks up on very subtle cues that other people send out. It's these seemingly invisible messages that draw us to one another and makes us fall in love, stay together and nurture love. They are also a big part of why we have trouble communicating, why we fight, fall into dysfunctional patterns or even break up.

The subject of this following book is, however, not uncovering these unconscious communication patterns. The following text aims to uncover and speak about verbal communication errors. The purpose of this book is to guide you through a couple of the most important communication mistakes. It will help you understand how you and your partner engage in these mistakes. It will also shed some light on where these mistakes have their origin and how you can spot them easily. It will also provide easy solutions that will help you nurture a healthier, more trustful and more harmonious relationship through communication.

Chapter 1. Expecting Things to Just Work Out

One common mistake we all make when it comes to communication is assuming that it is naturally given and therefore things will always go smoothly. We are all very different: our upbringing, role models, cultural backgrounds and psychological makeup make us unique. Sometimes the people we fall in love with happen to be very different from us. If you think of love as an opportunity to grow, learn about yourself and expand your horizons, then you probably understand that making a relationship work means a lot of work on yourself.

So what does this mean? Well, as children we do learn from what our caregivers tell us. But most of all we learn from the behavioral models we observe and copy, long before we can comprehend what is happening.

Some families have a habit of speaking a lot and placing a lot of emphasis on catching up. Some families never address their issues making an unspoken rule of keeping feelings for one's self. Other families might solve their problems by screaming and punishing while others might use humor as a mean to deal with any situation. Without even being aware of this, parents teach children how to operate in their future lives with all occurring aspects. As young adults, we might not even be aware of these behavioral patterns until we start ending up in situations where these old patterns just don't seem to get us to where we want to go. Sometimes, with a lot of luck, we might end up with a very insightful partner that has a great deal of understanding and manages to help peacefully navigate things. But most of the times our partners are just as "programmed" through their own upbringing as we are. So, we end up, depending on the situation in a war zone or cold and lonely place of isolated togetherness.

The good news is that by understanding the common mistakes people make when it comes to communication in relationships comes great hope and strength. The bad news is that changing yourself takes serious commitment and willingness to become vulnerable.

Chapter 2. Thinking There Is No Way Out

One of the most dramatic mistakes we all make is going straight for the quitting card. Yes, sometimes relationships throw us right in the middle of emotional storms; sometimes they leave us freezing in emotional wastelands.

Sometimes we might feel misunderstood, judged and powerless. In moments like these, it's easy to think about gathering your troops and beating in retreat. The role of emotions is a lot like that of bodily senses. Think of pleasure and pain for a second. When your body senses pleasure, it's actually telling you that what it's experiencing is "good" for it. When it's allowing you to experience pain, it's sending you a warning signal telling you that something is potentially threatening to your physical integrity. The same goes for emotions. When someone tells or does something that we perceive as "hurtful," we experience emotional pain. On the other hand, if someone does something thoughtful or pays us a compliment we experience pleasure. So, whenever something feels painful, our natural tendency is to avoid the person or situation that caused that emotion as an intuitive means of self-preservation. This is all good. Only things are not always that straight forward. Sometimes, pain, be it emotional and physical comes from our own subjective perceptions of reality, based on our personal history, traumas, and memories. So, in some situations, emotional pain might be a blessing in disguise. In relationships, this happens rather often. Because of the given closeness we share with our partners, we tend to have all our inner worlds mirrored back to us. In these mirrored images, we sometimes see things that we desperately try to hide from throughout our lives. Obviously, seeing our perceived flaws, wounds, shortcomings, and insecurities cause inner turmoil and pain. So, according to what our bodies are naturally programmed to do, we want to run or get away from whatever causes us pain as a means of protection. But this isn't always a very good thing for our personal growth or becoming.

One communication mistake we might make in such a situation would be avoiding the painful topic, trying to protect ourselves, not admitting our insecurities, giving in to shame, hiding our real feelings, lashing out at our partner for telling us the truth or even quitting the relationship altogether. So what you might ask? You might tell yourself that "the right person" would never hurt you. You might come up with all sorts of justifications that would help you avoid all the negative feelings. And this might work for a while. But the truth is that there is no right person. Everyone will hurt you, despite their wonderful feelings or intentions unless you make an effort, to be honest with yourself. Appreciate this honesty and take it as a real sign of friendship. Value it; make the best of it and take what you need from it in order to better yourself and your relationship.

So, if we're basically hardwired to answer in such a manner what can we do to avoid such mistakes?

There are certainly some strategies that are very helpful as long as you have the strength to stick with them.

The first and most important thing you can do is not respond to a tense situation in the heat of the moment. Unpleasant emotions sometimes cloud our reason, and we end up saying hurtful things. The problem is these things only perpetuate a cycle of "paybacks," resentment and guilt. Unfortunately, we can't take back things we have said or done, so it's important to think before acting. Also, remember that we always have a choice and it's our responsibility how we act in any situation.

Another helpful strategy is asking for second opinions. During complicated and tense situation, we might feel wrongly judged, abused, manipulated or hurt. We might end up questioning our entire relationship and our partner's intentions. In such occasions asking for an outside opinion might be of great help. The best choice would be seeking the opinion of a trained professional. A counselor or psychotherapist would be able to guide you through the sometimes confusing maze of relationship communication. However, this isn't always necessary. You can also seek support from your family and close friends. They know you very well, have a picture of your relationship history and dynamics and generally have your best interest at heart. However, family and friends might not always be the most objective people to address in such situations. You might want to consider just how much and what details of your intimacy you share with family and friends. Make sure that your partner would be comfortable with you sharing these details. Always think about what it would be like to be in their shoes and make sure you are as fair as you can. Present facts in an objective light. Focus on the problem, your feelings, not on pointing fingers and placing blame.

A great strategy in such situations is exercising your empathy. Always make sure you understand where your partner is coming from. You might experience unpleasant feelings during an argument or a tense time. First, make sure to give yourself a break. Acknowledge your feelings and sit with them. This isn't easy, but it's crucially important for your health and that of the relationship. If you need to, speak to yourself as you would to a friend. Give yourself a pat on the back for getting as far as you have in your relationship and for being a good partner or spouse and that you're more than able to find the proper solutions to solve your communication problems. Only after taking care of yourself you'll be able to exercise empathy with your partner. Are they snappy? Angry? Restless? Withdrawn? Instead of becoming angry with them for not giving you what you want or need why to ask yourself what's going on with them. If they're acting this way, odds are they aren't very happy. By doing your best to show empathy, support, and understanding you will gain your partner trust and respect. At the end of the day, it all boils down to giving what you would like to receive.

Chapter 3. Communicating Too Much or Not Enough

Avoiding difficult topic is a classic relationship communication mistake. Avoidance will get you nowhere. Relationship issues don't just get worked out on their own. By avoiding speaking your mind, you force your partner to push back their own thought, feelings, wants and needs. It takes a lot of courage to touch difficult issues, but it also builds trust and assertiveness. While not communicating is an obvious problem and the fact that too much communication can be damaging might come as a surprise. Constantly focusing on negative aspects, feelings, and outcomes is quite detrimental. Touching issues and deconstructing it all the time puts a lot of pressure on the relationship. It also takes the life, the fun, and the hope out of your couple life. Life is challenging in all its aspects. In order to thrive and make your dreams happen, you need to make a commitment to have fun and enjoy all challenges ahead. Do your best to balance out the serious and heavy stuff with light and fun activities and conversations. In the tense or conflicting situation, we tend to want to have all the answers and resolutions in order to rid ourselves of the unpleasant feelings. While this sounds all normal, it's not always possible. Conversations about difficult topics are tiring and consume emotional resources. Remember to take breaks and learn to listen to your natural rhythms. Commit to working out one problem at a time. When you're tired and stressed out, you might end up opening new difficult topics, putting more pressure on yourself and your partner. Let's say that you're not happy with the way your partner is spending money or helping out at home. After speaking about this if you bring up, for example, the issue of feeling less attracted to your partner, things might turn into a disaster. Difficult topics put a strain on partner's self-esteem. Bringing up a new hard to digest topic might break the other person's self-confidence and thus their ability to find the resources to deal with things.

So, how do you know when you're communicating too much or not enough?

Well, this delicate dance, just like any dance must feel a certain way. We each have different resources and abilities to cope with things. Make sure to dance with your partner and not against them. It's not an individual competition it's an exercise in cooperation. Like in any dance make sure the other person is fully there with you, giving their undivided attention. Also, make sure there are no other things on your minds. Be mindful of starting slow and clear. You each need to get into the other's tempo. Make sure you know how and when to lead and when to let yourself be led. If the conversation seems smooth, that's a great sign. If you can see a clear topic and outcome, then you are on the right path. Make sure not to put yourself down if you don't always get the steps right. Also, don't be mad at your partner for not being a perfect dancer at first. If you feel liberated, listened to, accepted then you're on the right path. If you feel constrained, criticized, put down, and aggravated, then take a step back and make sure to get all this out of the way. Learn when to stop or pause. If you feel tired, worn out, beat down listen to these signals and know that it's time to take a break or stop. If you find yourself being foggy, unclear, unable to focus, then it might be time to hit the pause button on that conversation. Make sure to listen to the signals your partner is giving you. If they also feel tired, unclear, worn out, make sure to give them time to breathe, think and recharge. You might feel good about finally hitting the topics that you needed to address. But your partner might feel overwhelmed. Don't be greedy. Make sure to treat them just like you would like to be treated.

Chapter 4. Making the Relationship a Target of Collateral Damage

When you first meet the person who you become intimately involved with, you are both separate people. You both have your own lives, your goals, your friends, your preferences. In time, with closeness comes a unique and wonderful occurrence. The two separate worlds inhabited by the partner's fuse and become a new territory altogether. When this happens sometimes, people get lost and need to find themselves within these new grounds. The danger here is not treating the relationship as the separate entity it really is. When we do or say things that don't acknowledge the existence of this blossoming third party, we sometimes end up hurting the relationship.

Think of this as a flower that grows from both partners' minds, souls, dreams, and values. Both lovers water this flower with nice gestures, trust, love, loyalty, and words. When a person's personal needs and values aren't met, they sometimes lash out on this growing flower. Yes, both parties must have their own separate lives that fulfill and make them happy. When we make the commitment of entering a relationship, we need to understand that there are great work and responsibility that comes with. This commitment involves taking care of the growing new thing that we create together. By breaking promises, taking advantage of our partner, not being supportive, keeping things for ourselves, saying or doing hurtful things we slowly and painfully kill the relationship. While these things aren't voluntary most of the times, it can be challenging to care for our needs, those of our partner and those of the relationship.

So, how can we properly care for the relationship and stop the potential damage?

One very useful thing we can do is speak about it. Ask yourself and your partner "What does our relationship look like? What is it made of? What values are its roots placed in? What does it need in order to grow and thrive? What am I doing right and what am I doing wrong? What am I doing that is hurting this growing flower?"

When the values, dreams, and goals of the relationship are clear, it's only a matter of acting in order to get things right. Many couples never speak about their relationship as a common creation. Instead, they focus on their individual faults, wants, needs and interests. This is a very common and detrimental communication error.

You might find usefulness in defining and uncovering your values to use a classic tool. Take the time to take such a quiz with your partner. Share your results and prioritize together, according to the results what your common and most important values are. You can even make a common drawing or collage that can represent your relationship as a plant. Place your common values with the roots in order of depth: the most important common values being the deepest and the less important being closer to the stem of the plant. Place actions and initiatives along the stem of the plant. Place personal and common resources as leaves. Place dreams, goals, wishes, and pleasurable outcomes as flowers. Make sure to add personalized items on your creation making it richer with time. This can serve as a map of your journey together that will give you a real reminder of the beautiful and delicate entity that is your relationship.

Chapter 5. Wanting To be Right

Power struggles are a real thing. There is a lot of energy between people who share the passion for each other and life in general. While this is a great asset and even a Holy Grail of relationships, it can also be a huge burden. When passion is not channeled in the right direction, it can turn your love life into a war zone.

When both partners are natural born leaders, it's sometimes hard to negotiate roles. Each person has their own view of what the relationship needs to look, smell, taste and feel like. While it's great to know what you want and what you're not willing to accept, having very strict expectations is very detrimental. Relationships are all about making us flexible in order to allow us to see new perspectives, become more creative and ultimately bring our unique joined contribution to the world we live in.

When we first fall in love, we see all the unique qualities in the other person and can't help to think of all the wonderful things we could do together. In time, we might lose side of this due to our rigid expectations and tendencies toward perfectionism. Instead of setting off to have fun, work together and merge our creativity we end up stopping altogether. "If it's not going to go my way it might as well not go at all." This is very hurtful and frustrating for both partners.

A good strategy to avoid this communication mistake is to commit just to do or create something together. Even if the outcome is imperfect, it's a great place to start improving. By not doing anything we sabotage our efforts and our growth as people and as a couple.

A great strategy to get over this communication error is to acknowledge our individual needs of control and commit to allowing change and flexibility. A good way to start changing these patterns is by choosing small tasks that are easy to manage.

First, divide the task into small steps. Let each partner pick what they would most enjoy and be good at. Negotiate these tasks and make sure you're both happy. Look at your individual strong and weak points based on your life history, education, passions, and results. If you need to, take the test that shows you skills, abilities, and talents. Set deadlines and evaluate your work together. If you need to, make sure to keep communicating and make adjustments. No matter what, don't allow each other to quit! Support each other during the project as you would do to someone you're not close to. Allow yourself and the other to be creative. Surprise each other and do your best. But most of all, don't forget to have fun and don't miss the point: you're learning to work together.

Remember always to stand clear of phrases such as: "I told you so!" This is very detrimental. Your partner already knows your point of view. If they face a setback that you've warned them about they are very well aware of this. By telling them you were right you're not showing support, you're merely sending the message: "We are in a competition against each other, and I won this round." Do the gracious thing and let the other person draw their own conclusions about who is right.

Chapter 6. Making Assumptions

Sometimes we feel like we know the other person like the inside of our pockets. This leads us to critical communication errors. We might know our lover, husband, fiancé or girlfriend more than anyone else. We might know what they are thinking without them needing to even speak. But this doesn't mean we know EVERYTHING. Every person is a vast and complex universe onto themselves. Each person is in the process of constant change and growth. To assume that we know everything; the feelings, experience and what they are about to do next is dangerous, and it is a big mistake.

Interrupting the other with a phrase such as: "I know what you're going to say" might be sweet when it is about picking dinner options. But in a tense or conflicting situation, this is a critical error that can lead to very strong arguments. When being told this, our partner is bound to feel misunderstood, hurt, boring and unimportant. When things are serious, and your partner seems to be in distress, make a note to yourself to take it seriously and understand their reasons. Make sure that both of you are calm. Take the time to listen to them carefully. Mind the words they are using and also observe their body language. Once they are finished, make sure you really understood what they're trying to communicate.

A simple strategy that will help you with this is by using formulas such as "If I correctly understand...," "What I get from you is..." Make sure to restate their sentences in your own words. This helps both of you set the ground for resolving an issue. This might seem pointless or time-consuming, but it is a great way to save yourself more grief down the line.

It's really important for all of us to feel accepted and understood by our loved ones. A good way of doing this is by assuring your partner that you understand what they are emotionally going through. In this situation, formulas like "I see that you're sad and I understand," "I can tell why this is frustrating to you...," "I can see that you're angry..." can be very helpful.

If you feel that what your partner is saying isn't matched by their use of words, their tone, actions or body language, gently point this out. This might be a great help in getting to the bottom of things. It also takes a great deal of diplomacy so make sure to assume a non-threatening tone. If you're not sure you got things right, you can always use clarifying questions.

Chapter 7. "Always", "Never" & "Why?"

Some words or phrases that we commonly use are really detrimental to communication in our relationships. When uncovering these traps, we might be surprised by the ways we've been damaging our relationship communication.

While "always" or "never" are very valid words, in relationship communication, they are pretty detrimental. How many times do we say things like "I always do all the work while you never really support me"? These words are important to be aware of because of the message they send out. First of all, these words don't really reflect reality. Even if in the heat of an argument it might seem this way, it's a given fact that our partner sometimes supports us or helps out. By using "always" or "never," we're invalidating everything our partner has ever done for us and the relationship. This leaves the feeling discouraged as their efforts are not valid enough or go unnoticed.

A good strategy to avoid this is by constructing your message differently. Instead of telling your partner "You never help out with the bills" you can say something like "I would really like it if you would help out with the bills more. When you do this, it makes me feel appreciated and supported."

When it comes to the question, "Why?" things look similar. "Why?" is a question that does not focus on really getting to the bottom of an issue. It doesn't seek clarification. It most likely seeks to point a judgmental finger in the direction of your partner. So, when you're asking "Why didn't you call me last night?" this implies they should have known you were expecting them to call and immediately puts them in a guilty position. Instead of asking "Why?" you can share what you were feeling in a more assertive way like: "I would have liked it if you called last night. When you don't call me, I feel unimportant and left out..."

Chapter 8. Criticizing Without Giving Positive Reinforcement

While in some situation we might feel like our relationship isn't all that fulfilling, it's important to have an objective evaluation. If we're willing to work through our differences and still have the feeling for our partners, the reality is that they must be doing something right.

In order to clear the air and work on relationship problems, it's really important to show our partner that we know that they are valuable and worthy of our love. If we focus solely on criticism and what we're missing, in the end, our partner will end up feeling like they are not enough or are unable to make us happy. This isn't the ideal place for improvement.

Make sure to show gratitude for the love you're sharing despite the imperfections. This not only helps our partner feel valued and loved, but it also helps us remember what we are fighting for.

A good strategy for doing this is keeping a diary. You can take a moment every day to monitor the progress of the relationship. Write down the nice, sweet things your partner did or said. Also, write what in their behavior inspired you to be a better person that day. Make sure to pick a day in the week where you share these things with your loved one.

Before sharing something that has bothered you or you would like your partner to work on, make sure to show your appreciation.

Remember, while it's ok to speak to others about your relationship, a huge communication mistake is speaking badly about your partner or putting them down in front of other people. If you want to pay them a compliment or praise them in public, that's altogether fine as long as it's sincere.

Chapter 9. Talking Down or Being Passive Aggressive

The way we address our lover or spouse creates a certain emotional climate. Sometimes the tone and the hidden messages say more than our words.

Taking down might be a behavior that we're not really aware of as it usually is learned from our parents. If this was consistently done to use while growing up, chances are we picked up on this hurtful behavior and are passing it on.

Talking down sends a message of being better than the other person, being superior, having more expertise or a superior intellect. Even if this applies in some situations, it's very hurtful and unfair and leaves the other person feeling inferior and put down. In truth, if we feel superior or entitled to talk down to our partner then we probably don't respect them, and we'd be better off calling it a day. If we're not really aware of in control of this behavior, a good strategy would be to start by being honest with ourselves and the other person.

A good way to do this is by asking your partner if they feel put down. Ask them to give you an example of such behavior. Identify when this response is triggered and why you're doing it. Apologize to your lover and ask them to help you change this by gently drawing your attention when you're engaging in this type of behavior. Look back at your past and identify who used to talk down to you when you were growing up. Become aware of these learned patterns in order to heal and change them.

A very common way of talking down to your partner that you might not be aware of is by giving the unsolicited advice or solutions.

Your husband or wife is not a child. They are capable of making their own decisions and surely are aware of the fact that they can ask for your opinion when they need it. Your need to give advice might come from a good place, but it is most likely to send out an unwanted message like: "I am worried about you"; "I think you're unable to do the right thing," "You are stressing me out" or "You are immature." By giving advice, you're putting pressure on the other person also to follow it.

Sometimes, you might be on to something or be entitled to give your partner advice. In such cases make sure that you ask for their permission and make your motives clear. Also, make sure you don't take it the wrong way if they chose not to follow it. Your partner is still the expert in their life and knows what's best for him or herself.

Remember to clear your motives with yourself first. When we love someone and share a life with them, their problems and questions tend to become our own. In order to get read of a state of tension of expectation, we might be tempted to offer the other person solutions that we find suiting. Make sure you clear the air about the pressure you feel or about your concerns that might have a toll on the relationship. Also, make sure you have your partner's best interest at heart.

While talking down is an upfront way of putting someone down, being passive aggressive is even trickier to deal with. We've all been victims of such behavior, so we are all in danger of doing it at some point.

So, what does being passive aggressive mean? Well, due to being unable to express ones-self while growing up, some people learn to say "yes" while they actually mean "no." They are thought in their childhood that they can never say "no" to the wishes of their parents or caregivers. So they bottle up a lot of anger. Later in life, they are still unable to assert themselves by gently finding a middle ground with other people. So they keep saying yes to everything, but their behavior speaks of anger, resentment and a denial to get to a common ground.

When being passive-aggressive, you appear to be nice and understanding while being quite angry, sad and resentful. You might also complain about being treated unfairly. You are prone to procrastinate frequently, especially on things other people ask you to do. You always find excuses and end up being surprised at how unfair others are by giving up on you. You act superior, distant and passive. You are late, and you often forget things, you make up stories, and you're very afraid of being seen as imperfect.

While this might not be you in general, when we encounter difficult times in relationships, when trust has been broken over and over again, you might be surprised to see yourself as being passive aggressive.

A good strategy to avoid this is by learning to be more assertive. Learn to accept your wants and needs. Gently communicate them and be open to negotiation. When someone loves you, they will do their best to keep you safe and happy so don't be afraid to communicate. This builds trust, respect, and cooperation. If you feel that you are quite passive aggressive make sure to educate yourself on the subject and see a mental health professional that will help you heal and improve your relationship communication.

Chapter 10. Projecting and Having Double Standards

You might hear a lot of advice about not changing for other people. The truth of the matter is that life and relationships are all about change. Whether we like it or not every encounter or relationship triggers change in us.

Being a leader isn't all about work or career. It's also a concept that can be applied in relationships and communication. Basically, being a leader means taking up the responsibility to be an example and to live with integrity. This means doing the right thing even if nobody is watching. This also means doing the hard thing when you have to. It also means being an example.

In relationships, being a leader means showing your partner that you can be brave, open, honest, hardworking, and considerate, or whatever else is important to you. This is by no means easy since it takes constant work on one's self. It also means constant communication with your partner. It sometimes means admitting to your shortcomings and taking action to improve yourself. While telling the person you love extremely helpful things, it's your overall actions and conduct that send a real message.

Most of the times we fall in love with people that mirror our inner world in a way that shows us what we desperately try to keep hidden. In such cases, we tend to project our shortcomings, weaknesses, and dissatisfactions on the person we love most. We might tend to point all these things out and ask them to change without being aware that we also need to face these facts. This might sometimes lead us into an endless dance of placing blame.

A great strategy here is to really be honest with ourselves. Whenever we ask our lover to change something about themselves, we must first ask ourselves "Do I also need to work on this?"

Chapter 11. Not Being Sober

Communicating might be hard. We all have our inhibitions, and sometimes alcohol and other substances seem to help with getting us to loosen up. At first, this might seem to work well but be mindful that this is both dangerous and unfair to your relationship. Healthy communication comes with work and effort. There are no shortcuts and no easy ways except for a change in perception. Instead of seeing things as difficult, think of all the ways these difficulties help you grow and heal. Also, focus on the positive outcomes and all the amazing things you are about to experience along with your partner.

Chapter 12. Interrupting Your Partner

In our day and age, with all the information, pressures and amazing things to do, we all have a deep sense of urgency that easily turns into crippling anxiety. In this context, we might be tempted to rush into things, say everything we have on our minds, accomplish everything we envision in a very short time-span. However, our excitement isn't always matched by the natural rhythm of the relationship or life's events in general.

In such situation, we might become unaware of our behavior and its impact. One common and seemingly harmless habit we might have is that of interrupting our partner when they are speaking. Whether we feel that they are too slow in expressing themselves, or that we are not comfortable with what they are saying, interrupting is detrimental to communication. When we engage in this behavior, we might make our partner feel like what they are saying is unimportant, thus making them feel disrespected in a sense. When interrupting happens often, overall communication might suffer. Our partner might not be so inclined to open up to us, and this is the exact opposite outcome from that of nurturing good relationship communication.

So how do we become aware of this communication error and how can we fix it?

First of all, it's important to cultivate the habit of drawing attention to this type of behavior whenever it occurs. Make an effort to draw the attention of your lover when they are interrupting you. Even if this is frustrating, try not to get aggravated or take it personally. Be gentle, respectful and patient. Interrupting might be a behavior learned by your partner long ago or something that happened to them quite often. Make sure not to let interrupting go unnoticed but use formulations such as: "I noticed that you didn't follow me through. Would you like me to continue?" or "May I please finish my idea, it is important to me that you listen to this." If you feel like your message didn't get through, make sure to inform your lover or spouse on your true feelings. Don't hold them accountable for their actions in a way that puts them down and make sure not to retaliate for your hurt feelings by calling names. Also, beware of making value judgments regarding the other person in such moments. The judgments might sound something like: "You're so inconsiderate for not listening to me." Instead, you can use a formulation such as: "Your behavior makes me feel like sad/ hurt like my thoughts or feelings don't matter."

Also, make sure that you use positive reinforcement whenever your partner becomes aware and makes an effort to listen to you. You can use a phrase such as: "When you listen to me I feel like I'm important and loved."

Chapter 13. Bad Timing

In an ideal situation, we would always be on the same emotional wavelength with our lover, husband or wife. In reality, this doesn't effortlessly happen all the time. This is, in fact, a blessing in disguise. Even the happiest couples are made of separate individuals with separate life stories, callings, and hardships. While communication and togetherness are truly essential, so is our time for introspection and unique pursuits. Only after deeply diving into our inner world, our work and our separate journeys and adventures we can truly be happy to reunite. It's this time alone that allows us to recharge, have tangible results and cope with the challenges that relationships pose.

Be attentive with your set and setting, just like you would when you dance. Make sure you are both relaxed, feeling good about yourselves and make sure you put all your stress and concerns on hold when you decide to talk. Carefully choose a nice place, a good hour for having the conversation you desire. No matter how pressured you feel by issues, don't write a wall of text on Facebook to your partner when they are in work, in an important meeting, out with their friends or at a family gathering. This comes across as disrespectful and immature. Your partner has his or her own life. They don't exist just to support you or tend to your needs. Yes, sometimes, you might feel abandoned, alone or stressed out when they aren't with you. In such situations, don't blame yourself and don't despair. But make a commitment to give them the alone time they need. Try to relax and also enjoy your own freedom. Take a relaxing bath, watch a nice movie, read a book, tend to your hobbies or pamper yourself. You can also go out with friends, visit your family or go out by yourself. If you need to talk to someone or have insecurities when your partner is not by your side, make sure to assess this issues properly. Instead of bombarding your lover with phone calls or text messages that are bound to ruin their mood, try a different approach. Speak to a friend, go on a forum for support or write in a diary. You can later communicate with your partner about the insecurities you are experiencing. If you are going through this, make sure to explore the issue. Learn where these feelings come from. Whether you were cheated on in the past, you are going through a rough time, or you are simply used to being together all the time, make sure you understand your insecurities. You have nothing to be ashamed of. Everyone has insecurities, but not everyone has the courage to deal with them maturely. If you find yourself having a hard time with these issues, make sure to see a mental health professional that will guide you through your healing process.

Make sure to always set a time with your partner when you can both come together and communicate.

Make sure you are both free, well rested and eager to spend time together.

Chapter 14. Being Impatient and Unnecessarily Demanding

Relationships are all about merging opposite things together in the harmonious expression of compassion and love. Old couples make things seem easy and smooth, but this seemingly effortless conduct is always the result of solid work. One important aspect of this work is getting your needs met while remaining unselfish. This process is a lot like dancing: one person leads, the other follows. Sometimes we end up stepping on each other's feet, stumbling, missing a beat, but that's ok. Learning to dance takes a lot of work, just like learning how to properly communicate does.

In order to succeed in this process, you will need to program your mindset properly. Remember, first, that neither you nor your partner can ever be perfect. That is what makes things challenging and beautiful. Also, remember that making mistakes is ok. Don't dwell on them. Instead, focus on all your victories, great and small.

Make sure to pay attention to your partner's natural rhythms, emotional expressions and general take on life. By observing them carefully, you will learn to read their moods and general emotional state. This is very helpful in learning how to properly choose your set and setting. If you or your partner are feeling tired, under the weather or have other important things going on, then it might not be a great time to communicate about important issues. In such situations, it might be wise to show your support for your partner in the same way that you would like them to show their support for you. Make sure you let your partner know that you are going through something so that they understand where you are coming from. Also, make sure that you understand when your partner is going through something so you can properly be there for them.

While life sometimes throws hard situations on our way, making your relationship a priority is important. If you and your lover have conflicting or busy schedules, a good idea is to set a day and time to reconnect. If you're in a long-distance relationship, this is also a good idea. Make sure the day and time work for the both of you. Remember to stand your ground without being selfish. Something might work for you and seem perfect but as long as it's not acceptable for your partner, convincing them to accept your point of view might be detrimental to the communication. By being cooperative, you show that you care for your loved one, respect the relationship and are able to compromise. These breeds trust and respect making communication and opening up easier.

Remember always to be polite. When you and your partner first met, you both probably made an effort to impress each other. The fact that you become close and intimate doesn't mean that you can forget about "please," "thank you" or "I am sorry." Remember to show integrity in any situation no matter how complicated or uncomfortable. The way you act behind closed doors is a real indicator of your integrity. Not being polite after winning someone over will give them the feeling that they were cheated into falling in love with someone that doesn't exist. Also, be mindful not to accept the same type of behavior from your girl/boyfriend or spouse. This creates a precedent that allows them to treat you badly and can even lead to serious dysfunctional behavior. It is also detrimental to your self-esteem leaving you feeling sad, unappreciated and unhappy. In such situations, you can firmly but gently point out to the other person that their behavior is unacceptable to you. Don't be afraid to assert yourself this way. If your partner loves you, they will understand where you're coming from and respect you more. The sooner you stop your disrespectful behavior, the better your relationship will be down the line. Remember your values and self-respect. Remember that you don't always have a say in what situations bring your way. But you always have the ability to take the high road and act in a way that will make you proud down the line. Before reacting, remember that one something you said or done that you can never take back. Also, make sure to be understanding and forgiving both to your partner and yourself. Sometimes we all act less elegantly than we would like it. That's ok as long as you don't dwell on it and make a commitment to do better next time.

In conclusion, communication needs to take into account the "when and how's" that work for both partners in order to properly bring you the results you want. Make sure it works for both of you, and it's not something done out of obligation.

Chapter 15. Falling Short On Commitments

In order for relationship communication to work smoothly, it is important to nurture trust.

When communicating closely and deeply, we need to know that we can trust the other person. Trust is gradually gained and needs careful consideration. Once trust is broken it takes a lot of work to rebuild it. Things that break trust are generally easy to spot.

A very important way of taking care of your trustworthiness levels is by always acting the way you would like your partner to act when it comes to you. Make sure to be as honest as you can. Of course, being honest doesn't imply being cruel or brutal. Make sure you tell the truth in a gentle, appropriate way. Don't say things that you do not feel just because you think that your partner wants to hear them. This will get you a lot of trouble down the line. Don't hide your true feelings, desires, and goals. Your partner has the right to know the real you. You also have the right to be known just as you are as you certainly have so many amazing things to offer. Make sure you're not very radical. For example, you might know that your partner wants to get married and have children. You might not feel up for this at the time. You might even feel like you're never going to be ready for such a commitment. You might be inclined to say something like: "Marriage is outdated, and I would never do this, I don't need a piece of paper to show my true feelings." This might be your true feelings at the moment. But by stating this, you come become harsh and disrespectful implying to your partner that their views and wishes are silly and outdated. Instead, you can formulate the same idea in a more diplomatic and considerate way such as: "At the moment I don't feel like marriage is something I relate to. My reasons are.... I understand and acknowledge your desires, but I can't promise you this." Make sure not to fall into the opposite trap. Out of wanting to please your partner and make them like you more, we might be tempted to "give" things that we're not able to follow through with. Don't tell your partner that you're also looking to start a family when you know that you're not. This will break trust and hurt feelings.

Make sure to come through with your promises. If you give your word on something or commit to doing something for the person you love to make sure to always follow through. If you can't do it or are not willing to, make sure to inform them respectfully. If you know that they are already relying on you, then do your best to keep your promise. Not following through is a great way to let your partner down and trust you less. It is also a very sure way to tell them that they don't matter to you. Also, if your partner opens up to you but asks you to keep the information private, make sure you do so. Of course, there are exceptions. But as long as your partner is a grounded, mature individual, make sure to respect their decisions and their privacy.

Always make sure to follow through with your promises and commitments, even when you don't like it.

At the end of the day, if you trusted someone with your affairs, wouldn't you like them to follow through?

Chapter 16. Being a Downer

Some of us are perfectionists. Some of us grew up with critical parents and caretakers. We might always ask the best of ourselves, and therefore of the people we keep close by. While asking a lot from yourself and others is a great thing, too much pressure and criticism can be more than a mood killer.

Think about what you would like to be treated like. Would you like your partner to fuel ambition in you? I suppose so. Would you like them to push you beyond your comfort zone and limits? Maybe so. Would you like them to take your goals, dreams, and aspirations seriously? Probably! In order to make this happen, you need to make sure you do it as well.

Whenever your lover asks for your opinion in regards to their results or creative pursuits, remember this is a great sign. It means that they value your opinion and think you are capable, intelligent and have good taste. Make sure you repay this gesture of trust with the proper reaction. Take your time to understand their effort carefully. Be honest. Don't butter them up or tell them that they are fantastic or perfect if you don't think so. Share your true feelings and opinions in a respectful, gentle way. If you not well trained in a discipline, not very inclined to appreciate art or plain clueless be honest about this. Make sure you are willing to learn something new and become interested in their passions or line of work. You don't have to become an expert. You just have to be open to listen to them and enrich your life with some new knowledge. This is also very important to understanding the person you love. It might seem pointless at first, but it most certainly isn't. A person's passions and pursuits tell us a great deal about them, their talents, the way they view the world and where they are in their life at the moment. So be willing and open to learning new things. Also, make sure that you share your own pursuits with your partner as they also deserve to get to know you deeply. Make sure you're not very critical or put the other person down in a harsh manner. The point of a relationship is to build self-esteem, not crush it.

Sometimes, due to our life experiences or even past events in the relationship we might end up holding grudges. In such cases, we might find ourselves being negative and having an overall "downer" attitude. If you find yourself in such a situation, make sure you attend to your negativity soon. Ask yourself what makes you want to put the person you love down? If it's your life experience, your parents, your teachers, your friends or your exes, then make sure you take the time to heal all of this. You can always read a lot and learn about how this behavior affected you. You can also work with a trained professional who can guide you and help you replace negative behaviors with new means of coping with life. This will certainly make you happier and better equipped to make your own dreams come true. Only in this mindset, you'll be able to be truly supportive to your partner.

If you feel like your partner is the one putting you down, don't take it to heart. Tell them how you feel. Be aware of phrases such as: "You are overly sensitive," "You shouldn't be feeling this way," "You need to toughen up!" or "Grow up!" Your feelings aren't right or wrong. They simply are indicators of what is going on inside of you. If something feels hurtful, wrong or right, then you should acknowledge that. Tell your partner that this way of addressing things is inappropriate and unhealthy. Make sure you make it clear that they need to respect the way you are feeling. Also, understand their motives for reacting this way. Due to the messages society and each individual family sends, we receive unconscious programming that sometimes proves to be detrimental to relationship communication. For example, men are brought up, in general being told that it's not ok to show their feeling. They are often told not to cry or be "too sensitive" because this is "womanly." Thus, without being aware of it, they might become adults who suppress their feelings in order to be "real men." This way, they don't allow themselves to truly open up that often and have a hard time being supportive because they simply don't know how.

A useful tool in these situations is uncovering what your unconscious drivers are. You can do this by taking an online test or seeing a psychotherapist who can help you uncover what you have been conditioned to do in certain emotional situations.

Make sure you never put your lover or husband/wife's dreams down. They might not be in tune with your own life goals or passion. They might even seem unrealistic or "silly." Keep in mind that this isn't your call. Who is to say that your loved one isn't going to be successful in their pursuit? Make sure to hear them out and keep in mind that they deserve to be happy, inspired and accomplished. Don't put your own interests first. No relationship can be successful if you or your partner can't experience the freedom to go for your dreams. A great way to do this is to encourage your partner to open up about their dreams and aspirations even if they are not sure of what they want or all the details. Listen to them in a supportive non-judgmental manner. Encourage them to speak their mind without fear. Help them formulate a coherent idea by asking open questions. Go from what they give you. For instance, they might know that they would love to be in the music business without knowing if they would like to perform or work in a studio. Ask questions to help them figure things out. Such questions might be: "Where did it hit you that you might enjoy doing this?", "What do you see yourself doing/working on?", "Would you work for someone else or be your own employer?", "Would you like to perform or support others in doing so?". Make sure to go easy on your loved one. It takes time to figure out what you want to do in this world of endless possibilities. On the other hand, encourage them to set goals and work consistently for their aspirations. Ask them if and how you can assist them in achieving their goals. Encourage them to get educated, network and seek outside support from people who are already accomplished in a certain field. Make sure your lover has a realistic life plan. Don't put them down but ask them if they have a plan for financially supporting their career pursuits. If they haven't figured out all the details, make sure not to pressure them but also not push them into a direction that might be detrimental to their quality of life. In such situations, it's important to guide your partner or spouse in the direction of their dreams without being too directive. They might take up your plans and solutions when they don't have all the answers. These temporary solutions might not be the best for them. Make sure they have all the time and space to figure their own path.

In some situations, your lover might have dreams and aspirations that don't really match their talents. This is a difficult situation to handle. You want to be honest with them, but in a way that does not crush their self-esteem. For example, if your better half dreams of becoming a visual artist but appears to be completely untalented, you really want to bring this up before they invest too much in something that will only lead them to disillusionment. A great way to do this is to motivate them to get in touch with someone who can properly evaluate their talent and skills. You can also tell them something like: "I know you're very passionate about your dream. I also think you have great talent, but you should maybe consider another career path that is more suited to your abilities. I am here to support you, and I just want to be honest and save you the disappointment. This is my opinion, and I encourage you to ask for other more qualified opinions."

Chapter 17. Making Comparisons

We all compare. We compare our looks, our achievements, our financial situations, our material possessions and even our overall value. This isn't good or bad. It's just the way we work. In order to establish how we feel about something, we need to compare it to another thing. The danger in this situation is when we get really competitive about things. A bit of competition in a relationship never hurt. It keeps ambition and passion alive. It also pushes the relationship and each person forward. However, competition can turn ugly and get in the way of love and cooperation. In such situations, we might compare the things we do, the amount of work we put in the relationship, the way we treat each other and our achievements. In such moments we might end up being frustrated, angry or ashamed. Whether we feel that we do a lot more housework than our partner or that they are showing a lot more excited about the relationship, this takes a toll on communication. In all fairness, we all need to feel that we have a partner who is equally able to carry the weight on our shoulders when needed. We are also very different. A good solution to handle this issue would be to clear the air. You can respectfully tell your loved one who you feel. It is very helpful to make a list of all house chores. Both you and your partner can pick tasks you are better at or enjoy doing more. Make sure to keep comparisons fair. Stand clear at all cost of statements such as: "I do so much more than you.", "You're lazy" or anything that says to your partner "I am better/abler than you." On the other hand, make sure not to put yourself down. You are just as valuable and deserving as your partner. Make sure to position yourself this way. Even if you feel like your partner is more accomplished and more appreciated, remember that you have your own individual life path, qualities, and challenges. If you are in a relationship with someone, be sure they have very good reasons to have chosen you.

As comparisons go, they don't always happen between the two partners or spouses. Sometimes we compare ourselves to third parties that seem to be relevant to our couple dynamic. Does it even happen that you pass by a good looking woman or men and compare yourself thinking about them? Do you ever think that your partner holds the same evaluations as you and thinks this person is more of less attractive than you? Maybe you sometimes feel like your partner thinks that their friend or co-worker is more charismatic or intelligent than you. In such cases, you need to stop. This might happen to you unwillingly. But this is unfair and has nothing to do with reality in a healthy relationship context. We all have insecurities. It takes courage to be open about them with our partners. But make sure not to burden your partner with your self-esteem issues. Make an effort to work with yourself and boost your own self-confidence. Treat yourself nicely, emphasize your qualities and work on the things you would like to improve. And always be kind to yourself. Self-esteem is the most attractive and useful mindset. No matter how you view yourself remember that someone loves you and has chosen you for your wonderful qualities.

On the other hand, make sure to stand clear of comparing your partner to other people. It's ok to be open and honest about your past but make an effort not to compare your partner to your exes. This will make them insecure even if they seem to come off better from what you are sharing. This type of behavior leads to lack of trust. If you're doing this with your ex, your partner will fear that you will engage in the same behavior with them. Make sure to stay away from comparing them with other people. A statement such as "My friend's boyfriend/girlfriend treats them so much better than you treat me" or "You know, my friend makes more money than you do" are very hurtful and detrimental to relationship communication. If you like someone more than your partner and feel like they have more to offer, then you're in the wrong relationship. Make sure to keep things between the two of you and not bring outside examples.

Also, make sure to NEVER compare your partner with someone else from a physical perspective. Telling your partner that someone else looks better, has a better nose, is slimmer or takes better care of themselves is really misguided and hurtful. Body image is always a sensitive topic, even for those with great self-esteem. Every person is beautiful in their own way. Comparing body types and looks only leads to insecurity, spite, and hard feelings. If you want your partner to work on their image, you can respectfully communicate this. You can tell them that you love the way they look with short hair, or that you find it really attractive when they wear suits or that you would love them to be fitter. Make sure that if you do this, you are willing to be open to your partner's opinions and wishes. If you find yourself comparing you or your partner's looks with those of other people, you might need to consider this as a serious warning sign. Seek outside opinion and even professional guidance if you are serious about the well-being of your relationship.

Conclusion. A Sympathetic Mindset

Well, dear reader, what I want to point out is that communication is a wonderful thing, but it can also be a genuine and deep struggle for every human being. Therefore, in order to understand and master communication, we need sympathy. Sympathy for everyone we ever communicate with, share ideas or fight. Sympathy for everyone who seems to get us so well from the first hello. Sympathy for that person who just won't pick up anymore. Sympathy for the person who you no longer speak to but think about all the time. And, most of all, we need sympathy for our lover, husband, girlfriend, partner or wife.

I would like you to kindly take a moment and think about all of this.

Think about the times you felt misunderstood, the times you felt like the person you love does not care, does not love you anymore. Think about the times you feel used or manipulated. Think about the times you feel like you're tired of talking.

Sit with these feelings for a while. They are normal, and a very fair price to pay for the many joys communication has given you. Also, be prepared to deal with them in the future. No real venture is without bumps in the road. Be prepared to take these feelings as important indicators of what is going on inside of you. Don't always understand these emotional states as indicators of what is happening in your relationship.

Also, please know that your partner felt the same feelings at times. He or she also felt powerless, enraged, sad, ashamed, guilty and misunderstood.

Do you understand now where sympathy comes into play?

When you feel ready, let all of these feelings go and make a commitment to yourself to choose what suits you from the following guidelines. They mean to serve you as a mindset intended to help you make the best of your reading.

1. Forgive yourself and your partner for not being perfect when it comes to communication. After all, you are a human.
2. Congratulate yourself for making this effort to learn more and better yourself.
3. Know that you are not playing against your partner. Know that they are not playing against you. *You are both playing together in the game of communication.*
4. Make it fun and creative! However, be mindful of the games you set in motion. Also, do not allow yourself to be played in ways that don't serve your well-being.

5. When it's not fun, don't make it tragic. Even when you feel sad, angry or powerless know that it's only temporary and you have the ability to express yourself in wonderful, creative ways that will enrich your couple life.
6. Have realistic expectations. Growth and learning take time, and they are intimately linked with many aspects of our lives. Observe all of this. Take your time. Allow the other person to have his or her own rhythm. After all, communication is a very subtle dance.
7. Write things down. When you set out in a learning process, your creativity might spark in surprising ways. You might want to share all your insights with your partner at once. This can lead to burn out and an opposite effect to that you're looking for. *Remember balance.*
8. When emotions are high, learn to take a step back and postpone important conversations. You have surely heard this before. And that's for a good reason you can never be warned enough about this. *Remember certain things can never be taken back!*
9. Be kind in communication, even empowering if you can. But never forget to be honest.

So, no real venture is without bumps in the road. I am convinced that you can start a happier relationship anytime. Why not start changing it right now?

Thank you for purchasing this book!

Olivia Lisenchi is also an author of "Woman's Guide to Fulfillment. Learn to Love Your Life." Please find it on her Amazon page.

Made in the USA
Columbia, SC
14 May 2019